THE WORLD'S GREATEST MOUNTAIN RANGES

GEOGRAPHY MOUNTAINS BOOKS FOR KIDS

Children's Geography Book

BABY PROFESSOR

EDUCATION KIDS

Speedy Publishing LLC

40 E. Main St. #1156

Newark, DE 19711

www.speedypublishing.com

Copyright 2017

In this book, we're going to talk about the world's greatest mountain ranges. So, let's get right to it!

WHAT IS A MOUNTAIN RANGE?

A mountain range is a geological area that contains a series of mountains that are grouped together. The mountains are connected and arranged in a line. Some mountain ranges are quite large and can be described as several subranges. For example, within the larger Appalachian Mountain Range is the subrange of the Smokey Mountain Range.

THE HIMALAYAS IN CENTRAL ASIA

The mighty Himalayas extend across the northeast section of India and cover a distance of about 1,500 miles. They extend through the nation of India as well as Pakistan and Afghanistan, and also a section of China, 75% of Nepal, and Bhutan.

The Karakoram Mountains of Pakistan and the Hindu Kush Mountains of Afghanistan and Pakistan are part of the Himalayan Mountain Range.

The range is actually composed of three subranges that are parallel to each other:

- The Greater Himalayas, the northernmost range

- The Lesser Himalayas, the ranges that are located north of Siwalik

- The Outer Himalayas, the southernmost range

The Himalayas

The word "Himalaya" comes from the Sanskrit, which translates to "abode of snow." After the ice deposits both in the Arctic and in Antarctica, the Himalayas have the third largest ice and snow deposits in the world. The range also feeds the Indus River, the Yangtze River, and the Ganga-Brahmaputra River.

The range contains over 15,000 glaciers. Other than the glaciers at the north and south poles, the Siachen glacier of the Himalayas is considered to be the second largest in the world with a length of 48 miles.

Siachen Glacier

The Himalayas are famous for their incredibly tall peaks. The range has over 100 peaks that rise above sea level to 24,000 feet or taller. One of the Himalayan peaks is the famous Mount Everest,

which at 29,035 feet in elevation, is the world's tallest mountain peak. Everest is located on the Sagarmatha Zone's border that separates the country of Nepal from Tibet and China.

Mountain climbers from around the world have attempted to scale Everest and K2, the second tallest peak, at 28,250 feet, which is a more dangerous climb than Everest. The amazing mountain peaks of the Himalayas are considered sacred by many religions including Hinduism and Buddhism.

Mount Everest Climbers

Snows of the Andes

THE ANDES IN SOUTH AMERICA

The Andes Mountain Range doesn't have the world's tallest mountains, but it is the longest of the mountain ranges on Earth. It stretches 4,300 miles in length from the north to the south of the continent of South America. The Andes Mountain Range is so massive that it's generally divided into three regions:

The Northern Andes, which is located in the country of Venezuela and the country of Colombia, and is made of three different ranges parallel to each other, eastern, central, and western.

Andes Ecuador

The Central Andes, which is located in the countries of Bolivia, Peru, and Ecuador.

Andes Chile

The Southern Andes, which is located in the countries of Chile and Argentina.

The tallest peak in the Andes Mountain Range is Mount Aconcagua, which is on the border that separates Chile from Argentina. It rises above sea level to a height of 22,841 feet. Just as the Himalayas influenced the cultures and religious beliefs in Central Asia, the Andes Mountain Range inspired the ancient South American cultures such as the Incas. They built their secret, isolated city Machu Picchu high up in the cliffs of the Andes.

Mount Aconcagua

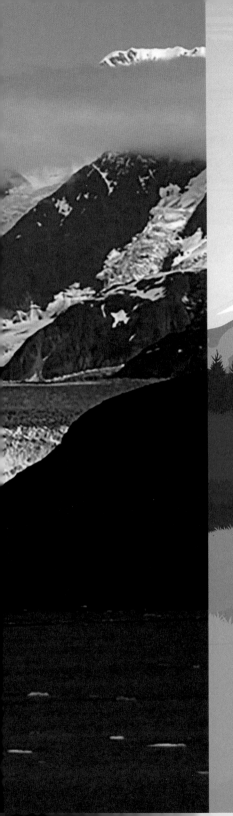

The Andes provide a huge barrier between the Pacific Ocean and the South American continent, so they have a huge impact on the region's climate. The range is home to almost all of the world's tropical glaciers, which are ice rivers that are permanent and remain unaffected by the balmy climate at the lower elevations.

Another interesting characteristic of this mountain range is its huge number of volcanoes. There are over 50 volcanoes that reach heights of at least 19,685 feet, and the world's tallest volcano, based on its above-sea-level measurement, which is 22,615 feet.

This volcano is the Ojos del Salado volcano, which is located on the border between Chile and Argentina. Its name "Ojos del Salado" means "eyes of the salty one."

Ojos del Salado Summit

Austria

THE ALPS IN EUROPE

The tallest mountain range in Western Europe, the Alps Mountain Range, sits like an umbrella separating the border of Italy from France to the west, Switzerland and Germany to Italy's north, and Austria and Slovenia to its east.

I t travels for a length of 750 miles and is more than 125 miles wide at its broadest location between the ski resort city of Garmisch-Partenkirchen, Germany and the city of Verona, Italy. The area it covers represents over 10% of the surface of Europe and it has a direct impact on Europe's climate.

Garmisch-Partenkirchen

North
Sea

Baltic Se

Masu

Oder

Vistula

Elbe

North European

Rhine

Harz

Ore Mountains

Sudetes

Oder

Elbe

Vistul

Ca

Bohemian Forest

Rhine

Black Forest

Danube

Panno

Danube

Alps

Plai

Sava

Po

Adriatic Sea

Dinaric Alps

Mediterranean Sea

The continent of Europe and the continent of Africa are colliding. Millions of years of pressure have pushed the mountains above sea level. It's hard to believe that the rocks located on some of the 12,000-foot peaks of the Alps were once part of low-level ground on the European and African continents. Some of the terrain at the highest elevations used to be part of the seabed!

The tallest peak in the Alps is Mont Blanc, which has a height of 15,771 feet. Other notable peaks all over 14,000 feet high are the Dufourspitze and the Weisshorn as well as the famous Matterhorn. The Matterhorn is located on the border separating Switzerland from Italy and is known for its pyramid-shaped peak.

The four distinct sides line up with the exact directions--north, south, east, and west. Many people have attempted to scale the Matterhorn

since it was first successfully scaled in 1865. Its steep slopes have claimed the lives of 600 climbers.

The Alps are a favorite European tourist destination. During the summer months, visitors go hiking and paragliding. From December through April, winter sports like skiing and tobogganing are very popular.

Paragliding

Many famous events have taken place in and around the Alps. In 219 BC, Hannibal marched his enormous army from Carthage across the Pyrenees and the Alps

in a battle against Rome in central Italy, which was one of the most famous military campaigns in all of history.

THE ROCKY MOUNTAINS IN CANADA AND THE UNITED STATES

The Rocky Mountains, also known as the "Rockies," are an enormous mountain range made up of over 100 different mountain ranges that stretch all the way from Canada to the United States. In Canada, the range extends along the border separating the province of British Columbia from the province of Alberta.

St. Mary's Lake

Then, it enters the United States and winds its way from Montana and Idaho down to Wyoming and Utah, then down to Colorado, and finally to its end point in New Mexico. The tallest

peak is Mount Elbert at 14,440 feet, which is located in Colorado. The mountain range stretches over 3,000 miles and creates North America's Continental Divide.

Water that comes down from the Rockies supplies about 25% of the water in the United States. Most of the mountain range is undeveloped and is protected by a group of national and local parks. Its high, jagged peaks are favored by mountain climbers and it's popular with tourists who love outdoor activities such as hiking and snowboarding. It's filled with beautiful vistas like St. Mary's Lake, which is located in Glacier National Park in Montana.

Upper Green River Basin, Wyoming

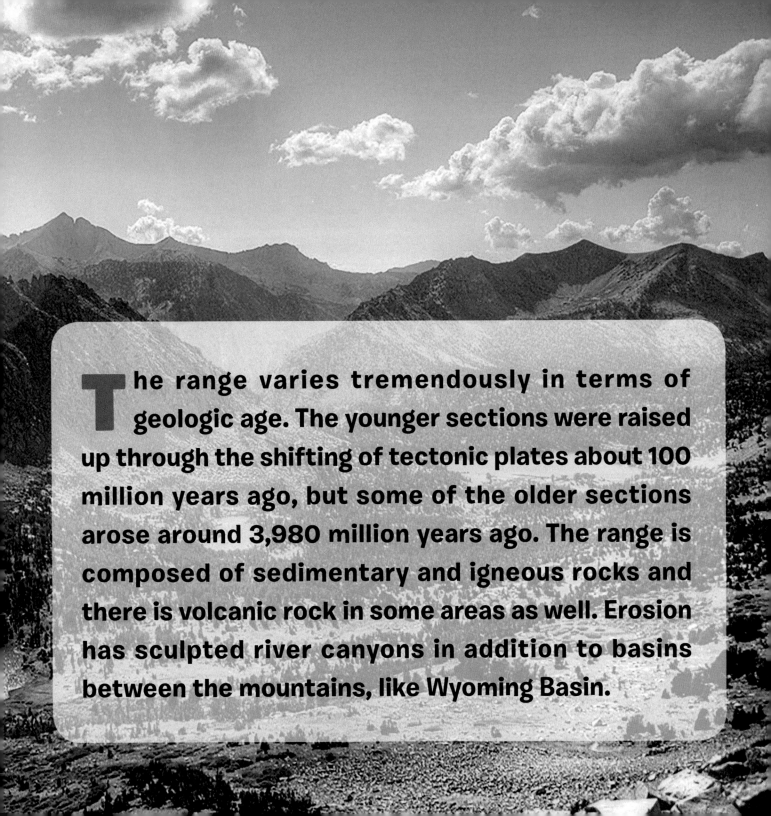

The range varies tremendously in terms of geologic age. The younger sections were raised up through the shifting of tectonic plates about 100 million years ago, but some of the older sections arose around 3,980 million years ago. The range is composed of sedimentary and igneous rocks and there is volcanic rock in some areas as well. Erosion has sculpted river canyons in addition to basins between the mountains, like Wyoming Basin.

THE SIERRA NEVADA IN THE UNITED STATES

The Sierra Nevada Mountain Range runs along California's eastern edge. It starts in the Mojave Desert and then stretches north to the border between northern California and the state of Oregon, where it runs into the Cascade Mountain Range.

Some of the most beautiful national parks in the United States, such as Yosemite National Park as well as Kings Canyon National Park, known for its Giant Sequoia Trees, are part of the protected areas of the Sierra Nevada.

Yosemite National Park

Pico del Veleta Sierra Nevada.

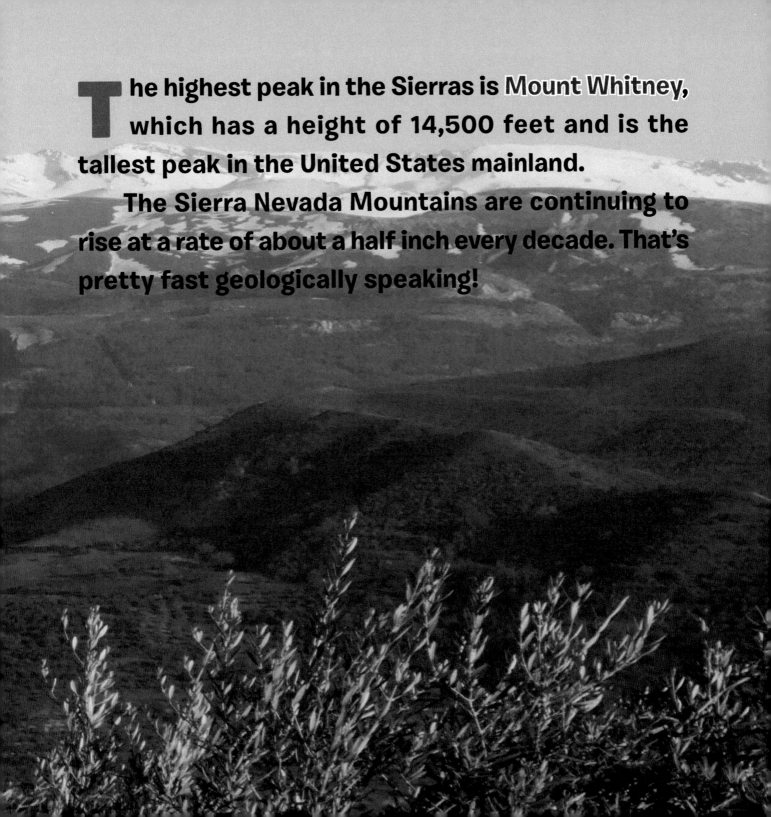

The highest peak in the Sierras is Mount Whitney, which has a height of 14,500 feet and is the tallest peak in the United States mainland.

The Sierra Nevada Mountains are continuing to rise at a rate of about a half inch every decade. That's pretty fast geologically speaking!

Mount Whitney

THE APPALACHIAN MOUNTAIN RANGE IN THE UNITED STATES

The Appalachian Mountains are some of the oldest mountain ranges on Earth. They were in existence before the continent of North America was formed. This vast system of mountains is a maximum width of about 300 miles and travels for 1,500 miles from Canada's Newfoundland and the region of Labrador to the center of the state of Alabama.

The highest peak in the range is Mount Mitchel, which is located in the state of North Carolina. It is 6,684 feet tall and the highest peak east of the Mississippi.

Awesome! Now you know more about some of the greatest mountain ranges in the world. You can find more Geography books from Baby Professor by searching the website of your favorite book retailer.

Visit

BABY PROFESSOR
EDUCATION KIDS

www.BabyProfessorBooks.com

to download Free Baby Professor eBooks
and view our catalog of new and exciting
Children's Books